Dingwell's Rules of Order For Email Meetings

By Tony Dingwell

Dingwell's Rules of Order
For Email Meetings

Copyright © 2018 by Tony Dingwell

ISBN: 978-1791555252

Dingwell's Rules of Order For Email Meetings
Table of Contents

Dingwell's Rules of Order For Email Meetings
Table of Contents

Dingwell's Rules of Order For Email Meetings
Table of Contents

Dingwell's Rules of Order For Email Meetings

1.0.0. Overview

**1.0.1.
Introduction**

Have you ever gotten up before the sun to catch the early morning flight to a meeting that lasts but a few hours and then return home late at night realising that you could have accomplished the same result through email? You bring up this point at the next meeting; everyone thinks it is a good idea. Unfortunately, you doze off because they serve decaf and awake to thunderous applause. They have elected the new chairperson, you. Everyone is interested in learning how your new email meetings will works.

**1.0.2. Email vs
face-to-face**

People often suggest this new kind of meeting as an alternative to face-to-face meetings. Participants prefer email meetings if they are spread about the country or the world where getting together for a face-to-face meeting is difficult and costly. However, when they try to apply the ordinary parliamentary rules of order, they soon realise that those rules no longer work.

**1.0.3.
Significant
assumption**

There is also one significant and necessary assumption for an email meeting, all the members of the assembly must have easy access to email. Such an access provision must be a part of the bylaws of any organisation that intends to hold email meetings.

**1.0.4.
Advantages**

Advantages of email meetings are as follows.

- **Participants need not travel to attend meetings.** Whether it is across the country or down the hall, people prefer the comfort of their own space to work. There is also the cost of transporting people to a meeting and providing them with refreshments. Email meetings can be a real money and time saver. They also makes it possible to work at home.

- **Scheduling a meeting is much easier.** Email meetings can start when you form or elect a deliberative assembly or committee and end when the committee delivers its final report or vacates for the next slate of members. No one can be unavailable for that length of time. If they are, maybe the committee should replace that member.

Continued on next page

1.0.0. Overview, Continued

**1.0.4.
Advantages,**
continued

- **Email meetings last longer.** An email meeting lasts at least several days as participants pop in to check their messages. Nothing prevents an email meeting from lasting years. A longer cycle between when a member introduces a motion and the vote gives participants a chance to reflect, research and record their thoughts leading to better decision making. You be surprised at how many decisions that face-to-face meeting overturned the next day when everybody has a night to sleep on them.

- **Participants can do other activities while attending an email meeting.** Not only can they attend other meetings but they can also consider multiple motions. However, they still must read their emails and respond when appropriate.

- **Dialogue during an email meeting is easy.** Best of all email meetings do not interfere with someone trying to listen to the person having the floor. All you have to do is send a statement to the chairperson so that he or she can send it out to all the meeting participates.

- **The computer can generate the minutes.** Have your minutes as detailed as you need, from a full verbatim of all email messages to short exacts of just the results. Now nobody is stuck with the job of taking minutes and trying to participate at the same time.

**1.0.5.
Disadvantages**

Disadvantages of email meetings are as follows.

- **Voting can be more cumbersome.** Email meetings face 10 different problems when it comes to voting on a motion. They range from verification of the authenticity of the voter to enabling a vote recount.

- **Confidentiality of the proceedings is impossible to enforce.** Any participant can save an email indefinitely and forward it to a third party at any time. Your security is only as strong as your weakest member. However, a similar weakness is also present when someone leaves printed copies of minutes of a face-to-face meeting on a desk or makes copies.

- **Using non-verbal cues.** Most people have difficulties communicating information commonly carried by nonverbal cues such as tone of voice, gestures, and expressions. Members who have a strong command of the written word have an advantage. The less spontaneous nature of email can also inhibit communication. However, this might be a good thing for those of us who have to sit through the long-winded.

Continued on next page

1.0.0. Overview, Continued

1.0.5. Disadvantages, continued

- **Backroom chatter.** The chairperson cannot stop participants from communicating with each other, whether that communication is part of the meeting or not.

- **Slow decision-making.** An email meeting can last longer than a regular meeting. So do not expect quick decisions.

Contents

This document contains the following sections.

2.0.0. The Difference between Email and Face-to-Face Meetings

Overview

**2.0.1.
Introduction**

We cannot use the typical rules of order for the governance of email or virtual meetings. For face-to-face meetings, we based the rules of order on the parliamentary model, which people have developed for oral communication among all participants. However, the virtual world is not the same as the real world; therefore, we need to develop a completely new set of rules to govern these meetings.

To use emails as the basis of communication among participants, we must first study the rules governing face-to-face meetings to discover their primary intent. Then determine how to apply them to the email meetings. Sure, we can do this through redefinition or extension of the meaning of a few of the words in the rules. However, to take full advantage of this form of meeting, we must throw out the parliamentary model and create new rules.

Let us now consider the difference between the email and face-to-face meetings and the changes we have to make to enable us to use emails.

Contents

This section contains the following topics:

Topic	See Page
2.1.0. Deliberative Assembly	5
2.2.0. Order of Business	8

2.1.0. Deliberative Assembly

2.1.1. Introduction

We must start with defining the elements of a deliberative assembly or the participants of the meeting. Recognising these elements would be simple in a face-to-face meeting, as everyone would gather in the same room. However, in an email meeting, participants may be scattered throughout the building, the city, or even the world.

2.1.2. Participants

There can be different classes of participants, from partial observers to full voting members. Therefore, we refer to anyone who is authorised to receive emails of the meeting as a participant.

2.1.3. Qualifications to participate

The nature of emails requires participants to have specific skills. These include ones that are in common with the face-to-face meetings such as command of the working language and the physical ability to attend meetings. However, email meetings also require participants to have access to email and the ability to work the email program efficiently. If you think your inbox is full now, think what it would be like being on a dozen email committees.

2.1.4. "Present" at a meeting

Typically "present" means being in the meeting room. However, the nature of email meetings is such that a participant need not be sitting at a computer terminal for the meeting to be ongoing. There can be hours to days when none of the participants are online because emails keep forever in the inbox unless they are deleted, unlike sound. It does not matter where a participant may be during a meeting. What matters is that the participant has access to email for the period of the meeting. Such access does not have to be continuous, but the participant should be able to check on the email meeting at his or her convenience and not miss any of the deliberations.

The email definition of "present" is the ability to follow the course of the meeting electronically and participate fully. Participants should ensure that they can fulfil these requirements before offering to serve on a committee that holds email meetings.

Continued on next page

2.1.0. Deliberative Assembly, Continued

2.1.5. Recognition of a participant

The visual aspects of standing or raising one's hand to get the attention of the chairperson to be recognised to speak do not apply at an email meeting for obvious reasons. Recognition at an email meeting is simple. Just send an email addressed to the chairperson is sufficient to serve as "recognition" for the purpose that is set out in the message.

Note that the chairperson does not have to assign the floor, or grant permission to speak to a single participant, as there is no problem with having people put simultaneous motions before the other participants at an email meeting. There is no need for participants to take turns, as emails do not interfere with each other as would happen with simultaneous speeches in a face-to-face meeting. The chairperson does have to keep close track of the various messages that members sent in and relay them out to the other members. The participants accomplish the discussion part of the meeting by the writing and transmitting of email documents addressed, quite literally, to the chairperson, and redistributed by him or her, most conveniently through the distribution list, to the participants.

2.1.6. Minimum officers

Because we do the business of an email meeting electronically, there is no need to have a secretary as an active member taking notes to produce a set of minutes. When there is a hand full of participates, the committee may be able to get by with just a chairperson. However, if there is a significant number of participants or very active debates, consider splitting the chairperson's role. It is common to appoint a speaker to handle the receiving and sending of emails and a teller to count votes.

2.1.7. Sitting

A "sitting" is the period over which the committee schedules its activities. For a face-to-face meeting, a sitting is usually a few hours. For email meetings, a regular sitting runs for a week with the first day dedicated to the introduction of motions and the last day for voting. Depending on the activities of the committee, a sitting could last longer say two weeks or even a month, and they can overlap with participants debating motions over multiple weeks.

Continued on next page

2.1.0. Deliberative Assembly, Continued

2.1.8. Quorum

For a face-to-face meeting, we based the quorum on the number of members present. Usually, a face-to-face meeting requires that at least half the members be present. For an email meeting, we base a quorum on the number of voting participants, as there can also be non-voting participants on the distribution list. Participants must assume that all with interest in the meeting's deliberations check their email for meeting material. It is the participant's responsibility to check their email and keep up with the discussions. Therefore, the participants are "present" at all times, and there is no point of order questioning the presence of a quorum at an email meeting.

2.1.9. Associated members

Non-voting associated members can enter into an email meeting and participate at the discretion of the chairperson. The chairperson typically provides this access when the associated members have appointed or elected the committee and require access to the deliberations. All the associated members need to do is request the chairperson to add their names and email addresses to the distribution list.

2.2.0. Order of Business

2.2.1. Introduction

Unlike a face-to-face meeting, there is no need to address 1 item of business at a time. Such a practice would be counterproductive given the length of time an email meeting can run. However, a committee must have a system to manage the order of business.

2.2.2. Throttling

Throttling refers to limiting the number of motions up for debate. In a face-to-face meeting, the chairperson has to limit the number of motions to 1. With multiple motions possible in an email meeting, participants could be faced with such a large number of motions as to render any sensible debate impossible. It is typical for participants to be limited to sponsoring a single motion at a time. This forces participants to pick and choose their motions wisely. If a committee needs a larger number of motions due to the nature of its work, then they should amend their bylaws to reflect a higher limit. If a participant requires a temporary increase in motions, the chairperson can grant this request through the suspension of the rules.

2.2.3. Order number

With multiple motions on the table in an email meeting, there has to be a way for participants to sort through their messages. To assist the participants, the chairperson assigns each topic or motion an order number on the subject line of an email that participants can use to sort messages. See 3.4.3. Subject line for the explanation on how the chairperson assigns these numbers.

2.2.4. Starting (and ending) a meeting

The chairperson need not give notice for an email meeting. These meetings tend to be ongoing or start immediately after the election or appointment of the participants. However, this does not mean that the chairperson should not clearly define the beginning and end of the meeting by sending out an email.

2.2.5. Call to order

An email meeting begins when the chairperson sends out the email to the participants in the form of a #Statement. The body of the email typically includes an agenda, and anything else the chairperson deems appropriate. The chairperson usually gives this statement the order number 001. This message is the familiar "call" to a meeting and is nothing new, other than the method of delivery. The chairperson uses this statement to link emails regarding general comments and discussions about the meeting.

Continued on next page

2.2.0. Order of Business, Continued

2.2.5. Call to order, continued | Where there are various lines of business or subcommittees, the chairperson may set up separate #Statements and giving them their order number at the start of the meeting. This practice makes it easier for participants to find information and report on various topics.

2.2.6. Addressing the speaker

There is one critical rule that carries over from the typical rules of order without change. Members must address only the chairperson or speaker. With an email meeting, "address" means that the participants have to send all email communications to the chairperson and only to the chairperson. To enforce this rule, the chairperson must not send out motions, questions and comments to participants if not addressed to the chairperson and with the proper subject line.

This rule is so critical because it eases the chairperson's chore of sorting out subsidiary motions from the general debate. More specifically this rule does the following.

- **Proper maintenance of distribution lists.** By having all official messages coming from the chairperson, using a distribution list, there is no need for individual participants to maintain and manage their list of email addresses. This list can be a problem if there are scores of participants or frequent changes in email addresses. The chairperson should confirm the addresses of participants before the meeting starts and when a participant requests an address change to prevent sending out confidential emails to non-participants.

- **Ensures fair treatment of participants.** A central distribution list eliminates points of privilege arising out of a participant not receiving an email, delays in receiving an email or emails sent to the wrong address by other participants.

- **Time stamping of emails.** Participants must send everything to one place to ensure the proper consecutive time stamping of a message. The timestamps ensure that the proper sequential recognition and precedence takes place for debates and motions.

Continued on next page

2.2.0. Order of Business, Continued

**2.2.6.
Addressing the
speaker,**
continued

- **Control the use of appalling language.** There is little that a chairperson can do to prevent a member from using unparliamentary language at a face-to-face meeting. (The chairperson can only remind a member or eject him from the meeting only after the member uses unparliamentary language.) However, a chairperson can refuse an email if it has offensive language and send it back to a participant explaining why he or she rejected the message.

- **Cleaning up the message.** While the chairperson must refrain from editing the words of participants, they must remove superfluous text such as quotes of other participants provided to help the chairperson slot the message into the right order. This practice not only reduces the number of distractions but also ensures that comments receive equal weight.

**2.2.7.
Adjournment**

Usually, the end of an email meeting would be set in the original call but could be extended or shortened by a motion. This rule respects the members' schedules and to ensure that all members have a chance to participate in a debate and to have their motions voted on without fear of a sudden adjournment.

In an email meeting, members check in on an intermittent basis; therefore, the length of the meeting does not constrain the members' schedules. Thus, there is no reason that a single email meeting could not go on for some weeks or even years. However, there should be limits to the length of an email meeting session. Typically, an email meeting session would either last from one:

- Face-to-face meeting to another;

- Reporting period to another;

- Chairperson to another or

- Period of election to another.

3.0.0. How Email Meetings Work

Overview

3.0.1. Introduction

In comparison to email meetings, face-to-face meetings are simple with members discussing one topic and a decision reached before the committee moves on to the next one. With email meetings, participants can debate numerous motions at the same time while having conversations covering many topics.

The reason for these multiple debates and conversations is the slow process of reaching a decision. A face-to-face meeting can reach a decision anywhere from a few minutes to several hours. However, where an email meeting runs on a sittings schedule, the earliest time that a committee can reach a decision is at the end of a sitting when the chairperson has counted all the votes for the motions. Having several motions and discussions going on at the same time speeds things up at an email meeting.

Contents

This section contains the following topics:

3.1.0. Handling Motions (the Chairperson's Job)

3.1.1. Introduction

The management of an email meeting is a challenge at the best of times. Chairing such a meeting when the meeting body is large, active, and contentious can be overwhelming.

How can a chairperson conduct an email meeting without burning out? The key lies in the time stamping of the email. Just as in a face-to-face meeting where the chairperson recognises the first person to rise to make his or her motion, debate next, or make an amendment. The timestamp determines who is next in line at the email meeting, and the gatekeeper is the chairperson.

3.1.2. Handling motions (automation)

While a computer program or system can do some of the chairperson's role, much of it still is still a matter of judgment. Designing a program to "run" email meetings, would involve some rather strict format rules. Unless your organisation has the funds for such a service, it may be best if the chairperson handles motions manually.

3.1.3. Simple main motions

To make a motion, a member would word the motion and send it directly to the chairperson identifying it as regarding the meeting. By directly, I mean without the member sending copies to other members. This rule protects participants from members bombarding each other with emails or left out of the debate because someone forgot to update their mailing list. It also allows the chairperson to reject the motion if it is out of line or contains unparliamentary language.

3.1.4 Motion vs submission

The motion could also come by way of submission. A submission is a document that a committee is required to address either as part of their mandate or by convention. Examples of submissions include reports from subcommittees and applications requiring the committee's approval.

If the motion is in the form of a submission, the chairperson sends it out with the standard motion to accept the report or application.

Continued on next page

3.1.0. Handling Motions (the Chairperson's Job), Continued

3.1.5. Seconding a motion

An email meeting does not require a seconder for a motion to be debated. Seconding helps to weed out motions intended to run out the clock on a meeting. As an email meeting can deal with multiple motions at the same time and can continue for days or weeks, frivolous motions are not a problem. They are just defeated.

It is still possible to bog down an email meeting with excessive motions. To prevent this from occurring participates are usually limited to having 1 motion on the table. The committee could raise this limit depending on the nature of the meeting. Also, committees can place caps on the number of submissions with rules as to which ones receive priority.

3.1.6. Not so simple main motions

You would think that any amending, privileged, or incidental motions would result in the suspension of debate on the main motion like what happens in a face-to-face meeting. This could easily be done because the timestamp on each message would allow the chairperson to sort everything out on a first-come-first-served basis, with allowances for legitimate debate that members send in before receiving the new motion.

For example, suppose a motion to amend the main motion shows up, followed by more discussion messages dealing with the main motion, the time-stamps guide the chairperson's actions on the amendment message. The chairperson could set aside any discussion on the main motion that arrived after the amendment, which would be out of order in a face-to-face meeting, but not delete them. Then send out the amendment and ask the members to focus their debate on the amendment. The chairperson would return any debate messages on the main motion to the originators with a note of explanation stating that the message was out of order at the time sent. If the amendment was defeated, the chairperson could transmit out any main motion debate that came in earlier. If adopted, the motion would have changed, making the debate irrelevant and the chairperson would return all earlier debate emails with a note explaining that the motion has been amended and inviting the participant to resubmit if they think that their comments are still relevant.

The problem with suspending debate is that someone could use this procedure to delay the vote on the final main motion to the next sitting and if the committee amends that motion, then there is another delay. This could allow someone to delay a vote indefinitely.

Continued on next page

3.1.0. Handling Motions (the Chairperson's Job), Continued

3.1.6. Not so simple main motions, continued

The solution to this problem is to allow members to vote on the amendment along with the main motion. This prevents someone from amending a motion to create a delay. To prevent an amendment from changing the substance of the main motion, the chairperson must apply any votes cast for an amendment that fails to gain a majority to the main motion. No votes can be cast against an amendment only the main motion. Also, because of the email meeting rule that a maker of a motion must vote for a motion, it is not a good idea to amend a motion in an effort to defeat it because it creates a second vote for the main motion.

3.1.7. Other motions

Because email meetings allow multiple motions to be on the table and use sittings to manage time, some motions used in face-to-face meetings are either not necessary or need translation for email meetings.

3.1.8. Obsolete motions

Here is a list of motions that are no longer necessary.

- **Motion to Adjourn** – Since participants cannot end email meetings before their closing date as announced in the call, this motion is not appropriate.

- **Motion to Recess** – Since participants do not miss any of the meetings if they take a break from their computer, we do not need this motion.

- **Limitations on Debate** – The length of debate messages is self-enforcing as participates would skip over or deletes messages that look too long to bother reading. The same is true about a large number of messages coming from any 1 person. Also, since email messages can be short, the number of them from a single person should not be limited as it may take a multi-message exchange to get the point across. Anyone can skip repetitions emails once their meaning is clear.

- **Object to Consideration** – The requirement to make the motion before any debate begins is self-enforcing because if a participant does not submit the motion at the beginning of a sitting, there is no possibility of a vote at the end of a sitting.

- **Lay on the Table** – Would have no application for an email meeting does not need to be interrupted for an "important" and time-critical issue. If members have to do something important, they can go and do it, and catch up with the debate messages later.

Continued on next page

3.1.0. Handling Motions (the Chairperson's Job), Continued

3.1.8. Obsolete motions, continued

- **Orders of the Day** – A call to adhere to the agenda would not be necessary as participants can debate all motions during a sitting.

- **Limit Debate** – Closing debate at a particular time or limiting the time for debating is not an issue because the sittings of an email meeting determine the time of the vote.

- **Postpone to a Certain Time** – Stating a time to resume debate the motion or agenda item is not applicable since multiple motions and agenda items can be on the table at the same time.

- **Take From the Table** – Temporarily suspending further consideration on the pending question is not necessary as there can be multiple motions on the table. Therefore, removing a motion that has no chance of passing cannot speed up the meeting.

- **Reconsider** – To change position or view would require another main motion.

- **Postpone Indefinitely** – Killing the question or resolution has no benefit.

- **Previous Question** – Closing debate has no benefit.

- **Informal Consideration** – Moving that the assembly go into "Committee of the Whole" is not applicable. Members can continue to discuss a motion right up until the chairperson calls for a vote.

3.1.9. Motions requiring alternative handling

Here is a list of motions that require alternative handling.

- **Appeal from the Ruling of the Chairperson** – Is a motion that deserves a special note, as such a motion would be a time-critical issue. Opponents of the motion could introduce excessive delays by raising points of order and then appealing. Thus extending the consideration of the motion past the time of its usefulness unfairly, as the majority would not get to have their say. A solution is to have an arbitrator receive all appeals, with the decision to be binding. The arbitrator would promptly reach his or her decision independent of the on-going meeting. The mere existence of this appeals procedure would go far to deter frivolous points of order and appeals intended to cause delay.

- **Point of Privilege** – Issues involving the tone of the meeting should be prevented by the chairperson when reviewing the incoming emails.

Continued on next page

3.1.0. Handling Motions (the Chairperson's Job), Continued

3.1.9. Motions requiring alternative handling, continued

- **Parliamentary Inquiry** – The chairperson should quickly resolve inquires as to the correct motion to accomplish the desired result, or raise a point of order should be quickly resolved by the chairperson.

- **Point of Information** – Generally applies to the information desired from the speaker: "I should like to ask the (speaker) a question." The chairperson should quickly resolve points of information.

- **Point of Order** – Infraction of the rules or improper decorum in speaking should be prevented by the chairperson when reviewing the incoming emails.

- **Divide the Question** – Dividing a motion into 2 or more separate motions that are independent of each other can be done by the chairperson on request of a member as members in disagreement can vote for or against all of the split motions. However, caution should be exercised since splitting the motion automatically results in another vote being cast for the motion.

- **Consider by Paragraph** – The chairperson can handle the request to withhold the adoption of a paper until all paragraphs are debated and amended, and the entire paper is satisfactory by dividing the paper into paragraphs for discussion and approval.

- **Amend** – The chairperson can insert or strike out words or paragraphs, or substitute whole paragraphs or resolutions if the participant who made the motion agrees. If not, as the participant proposing the amendment could have put forward an opposing motion for consideration.

- **Withdraw/Modify Motion** – A mover can withdraw a motion or accept an amendment.

- **Commit /Refer/Recommit to Committee** – Referring the question or resolution to another committee can only be done through a main motion, as the length of a sitting should provide ample time to consider most motions.

Continued on next page

3.1.0. Handling Motions (the Chairperson's Job), Continued

3.1.9. Motions requiring alternative handling, continued

- **Extend Debate** – Applies only to main motions and extends debate for one more session. When requested by a member, the chairperson adds 'extend debate' as a voting option. If the votes for the main motion make a majority, then the main motion is carried. If the votes for the main motion and extension make a majority, then the debate is extended. If the votes against the motion and the votes for the extension make a majority, then both the motion to extend and the main motion are defeated. The votes for extension are presumed to be against the main motion as the only reason to vote to extend the debate would be to wait for additional information that could result in the participant changing his or her mind and vote for instead of against the motion.

- **Object to Consideration** – A participant must state his or her objection before discussion or before someone makes another motion. The chairperson should review motions and the proposers advised of questionable ones, as they would likely be defeated when the issue comes up in the debate.

- **Suspend the Rules** – The chairperson can consider allowing an assembly to violate their rules of order (except the Constitution), but the benefits of suspending the rules must be significant.

3.2.0. Moderating Debate

3.2.1. Introduction

There would be no need to "recognise" individual members to speak in the debate, because "simultaneous" emails would not create chaos, as would simultaneous speeches.

3.2.2. Options

If there are no subsidiaries or incidental motions, the chairperson could moderate the debate in several ways. The simplest would be to base the discussion on the timestamps. Individual emails containing comments or questions would arrive in the chairperson's inbox, edited to remove excess information and assigned the correct subject line with tag. Then the chairperson sends it out through the distribution list in the order of the time he or she receives the messages.

The chairperson could also delay sending out messages for a short period after the initial motion to give an opportunity for participants to express their opinions without the influence of others.

The chairperson could also interleave messages when sending them out, into alternating pro and con arguments. However, this may not be necessary, as the receiver of the messages would most likely get them in batches, and could read the message the order he or she pleases.

This resending of messages could probably happen automatically as the chairperson should not take it upon him or herself to edit or hold back messages, except to remove redundant information such as quotes from another participant or the use of unparliamentary language. If the chairperson did edit a message, the sender of a message would be watching for it to come back and would quickly catch the difference.

3.2.3. Message size limits

There could be a rule put in place to limit individual emails to no more than 1,000 words or so, in the same way, speaking to a motion is limited to N-number of minutes. However, such a rule is not essential to the mechanics of running an email meeting where a "short message" rule is self-enforcing. If an email is too long, a participant may not bother to read it. One does not have this choice if a speech is too long. Too bad the delete key does not work in a face-to-face meeting. Therefore, if debaters want participants to consider their points, they should keep their messages short.

Continued on next page

3.2.0. Moderating Debate, Continued

3.2.4. Voting results	Once the members vote, the chairperson would send out the results in the form of a communiqué that would also form the minute for that motion.
3.2.5. Out of order motions	If a member sent in a motion that was clearly out of order, the chairperson should return it to the originator with an explanation. For example, a subsidiary motion at a lower level than the pending motion.
3.2.6. Points of order	If a member sent in a legitimate point of order, the chairperson would allow it to interrupt the proceedings (as in a face-to-face meeting), and the chairperson would send it out to all with his ruling. "Interrupt," in this context, means that incoming messages would be set aside and held until the chairperson settles the point of order. If a participant does not appeal the ruling after an appropriate time interval, the chairperson resumes the transmission of any accumulated messages on the same first-in-first-out basis as before. If there were an appeal, the chairperson would wait for a decision of an arbitrator.
3.2.7. Trade-offs (cost vs time)	The use of email to hold meetings to save substantial amounts of money for travel, meals, and lodging, while gaining the convenience of attending in pyjamas, and increasing participatory democracy, one has to pay for that by the expenditure of time. At least the amount of time spent in the "meeting" that is to say, sitting at a screen reading and writing an email, would probably be less than the total time spent at a face-to-face meeting in a distant city, but not half as much fun!

3.3.0. The 10 Voting Problems and How They Are Solved

**3.3.1.
Introduction**

Any good voting system (Internet, email, or otherwise) has several characteristics to assure that those tabulating the vote properly translate the wishes of each voter. These are as follows.

Essential

1. *Authentication* – the person voting is who he or she says.

2. *Authorisation or registration* – the person voting is an actual member.

3. *Anonymity* – the ballot is secret and stays that way.

4. *Indecision* – a voter changing his or her vote before he or she finally casts it.

5. *Permanence* – a vote, once a voter finally casts his or her vote, no one should alter it.

6. *Uniqueness* – a person cannot vote more than once, or cast duplicate votes.

7. *Audit* – assurance that a scrutineer did count the votes, and someone else can recount the votes, if necessary.

Nice to Have Characteristics

8. *Documentation* – who voted, and who did not, as a public record. The courts hold each member liable for motions that are illegal or reckless actions. The justice system excludes members who vote against such motions from prosecution. Therefore, it is a good idea to be able to determine who voted for and against in the case of such motions.

9. *Verification* – the voter can discover if his or her vote has been changed or miscounted and fix it without destroying the secrecy of the ballot.

Problems Unique to Email Meetings

10. *Simplicity* – the voting operation should be simple to carry out, particularly for an unsophisticated computer user.

Continued on next page

3.3.0. The 10 Voting Problems and How They Are Solved, Continued

3.3.2. Solution	The solution is simple. Appoint a trusted member to conduct the voting process. For more formal or sensitive meetings, a committee could engage the services of a third party teller such as an independent registered or certified parliamentarian. Using a teller solves the 10 voting problems as follows.

1. *Authentication* – The committee can authorise the teller to perform some authentication procedures, such as giving each member a code in advance of the first vote that only the member and the teller know, or simply calling the voter and asking enough questions to verify identity. These are only 2 ways; others are possible.

2. *Authorisation or registration* – The teller has been given a list of names with email addresses in advance of the meeting and verify as in problem #1.

3. *Anonymity* – Only the teller knows for sure, and reports only the numbers in electoral votes.

4. *Indecision* – A voter can revote any time before the deadline, and the teller verifies as above.

5. *Permanence* – The teller accepts no more votes not "in the system," or sent by a given time.

6. *Uniqueness* – The verification process takes care of voting more than once, and you have to trust the independent professional or certified parliamentarian who is acting as the teller to ensure that someone does not copy his or her vote.

7. *Audit* – Here is a case where registering your abstention is necessary, so the number of votes + abstentions should add up to the number of voting members. The teller can verify by email or phone with any member who did not vote or register an abstention.

8. *Documentation* – The teller can produce a list of members who voted or abstained and submit it to the secretary for inclusion in the record.

9. *Verification* – By communicating directly with the teller by email or phone, members can verify that the teller had received their votes.

Continued on next page

3.3.0. The 10 Voting Problems and How They Are Solved, Continued

3.3.2. Solution,
continued

10. *Simplicity of process* – The voter could "phone it in" to the teller, or the teller could email the voter, and the voter replies to the teller's email.

3.3.3. Process

This table outlines the voting process using a teller.

Stage	Description
1	The chairperson would notify (presumably by email) the teller that a vote is in process on the motion to (fill in the blank), and all votes must be to the teller by a given time.
2	The chairperson notifies participating members to send their electronic votes to the teller by a given time.
3	The teller receives and tabulates the votes and makes a teller's report to the chairperson.
4	The chairperson sends an email announcing the results.
5	Vote completed.

3.4.0. Message Conventions for Email Meetings

3.4.1. Introduction

Knowing how to properly format and send an email for a meeting is essential to participating in an email meeting. While the chairperson is responsible for sending out official emails to members, how you write your email can make a big difference as to how efficiently he or she can do his or her job. This section outlines how to prepare an email that a chairperson can easily process for redistribution.

3.4.2. Addressing

Always send emails that you want to have included in the official transcripts of the meeting to the chairperson and only to the chairperson for the following reasons.

1. You must address and send all official emails for the meeting to the chairperson and only to the chairperson. The chairperson must reject any emails that you have carbon copied to others as invalid.

2. The chairperson may have set up a filter within his or her email application to sort emails so that he or she can give priority to official emails and ignore the unofficial.

3.4.3. Subject line

People sitting on many committees that conduct e-meetings receive a large volume of emails. To keep their inboxes organised they would set up inbox rules within their email applications for the sorting of the meeting messages. It is critical that the chairperson can identify these messages. To accomplish this, they use a distinctive subject line. Therefore, the chairperson needs to know and use the naming convention approved by the committee. An example of a subject line is as follows.

ABC-X-2012-123: #Report - Financial Statements 2012-03-31

Where:

- *ABC* – Identifies the organisation (ABC Corporation). Remember, people may also be participating in many meetings for different organisations at the same time.

- *X* – Identifies the committee (Executive Committee). It is typical to use single letters for senior or standing committees, and double or triple letters for a sub or ad-hoc committees.

Continued on next page

3.4.0. Message Conventions for Email Meetings, Continued

3.4.3. Subject line, continued

- *2012* – Identifies the committee's session. The year or a serial number indicates the session.

- *123* – Identifies the order (individual main motions) and statements (discussion threads) that eventually become part of the minutes.

- *#Report* – This is the tag. It identifies the purpose of the message (Report).

- *Financial Statements 2012-03-31* – A description of the discussion at the end provides additional information.

3.4.4. Tags

Tags are helpful to tell what an email is trying to address. They are placed in the subject line of the message and are always a single word beginning with an # so that it can be identified and handled by an inbox rule. Typical tags and the order in which they would appear are as follows.

For Statements

- *#Statement* – The message is the opening statement of the session or discussion thread.

- *#Report* – The message is (or contains as an attachment) a report. When sending a report as an attachment, it is proper to give a summary of the report in the body of the message.

- *#Comment* – The message is a comment on a statement.

- *#Communiqué* – The message is a summary of the session prepared by the facilitator. Summaries of long sessions are helpful so that members know what the committee has accomplished and what they still need to consider.

- *#Final* – The message is the final communiqué of the session. It formally closes the meeting by summarising all the results, thereby creating the minutes of the meeting.

Continued on next page

3.4.0. Message Conventions for Email Meetings, Continued

3.4.4. Tags, continued

For Motions

- *#Motion* – The message contains the motion.

- *#Question* – The message is a question on the motion

- *#Against* – The message speaks against the motion.

- *#For* – The message speaks for the motion.

- *#Vote* – The message contains instructions on voting.

- *#Results* – The message contains the results of the vote prepared by the teller. Also, the chairperson issues a separate minute, which also records the result of the vote. The reason for this apparent duplication is to official document the chairperson's declaration of the results. Also, there is the possibility that the vote could be inconclusive as in the case where the members vote to extend debate on the motion.

4.0.0. Roles

Overview

**4.0.1.
Introduction**

The roles and responsibilities of the various members of an email meeting differ slightly from that of members who meet face-to-face. This section looks at the roles played by the following.

- The chairperson with the sub-roles of:
  - Speaker
  - Secretary
  - Teller
  - Premier

- The participants

Contents

This section contains the following topics:

4.1.0. The Role of the Chairperson

**4.1.1.
Introduction**

With a small committee with a light workload, a chairperson could handle all aspects of the meeting. Larger committees with heavier workloads can break up the work of chairperson to the following officers.

1. Speaker — This officer receives and recognises all messages.

2. Secretary — This officer prepares the minutes.

3. Teller — This officer or a third party conducts the voting.

4. Premier — This officer is the senior participant responsible for ensuring that the committee completes its mandate.

These officers could also appoint deputies to assist them or fill in when they are not available. It would be possible to have several deputy speakers to ensure coverage 24/7.

4.1.2. Speaker

This table outlines the actions of chairpersons in their role as speaker.

Step	Action
1	Receives emails from participants.
2	Determines if the email is in order.

If it is...	Then the chairperson...
In order	Forwards the email to the participants without comment, except to change the subject line or add a tag and to remove the original message from a reply.
Not in order	Returns message to the sender with an explanation. Typical reasons for a submission not being in order are: ■ Missing the deadline ■ Use of unparliamentary language

TIP: When dealing with busy committees, speakers should consider keeping themselves organised by using inbox rules to sort and file emails

4.2.0. The Role of Secretary

4.2.1. Introduction	This table outlines the actions of chairpersons in their role of secretary to prepare minutes.

Step	Action
1	Copies the emails into a single document.
2	Edits the document for readability by correcting: • grammatical errors • spelling
3	Prepares the minute, which highlights the committee's resolution of the motion.
4	Submits the results.

4.2.2. Minutes	The minutes for an email meeting are the emails themselves copied and pasted into a document. This document can be huge, so the secretary may use the discussion threads to break it into sections. Also, the secretary may place a summary at the beginning of the minutes of the threads using the #Results and #Communiqué statements.

4.2.3. Approval of minutes	This table outlines the process for approving the minutes.

Stage	Description
1	The secretary emails a copy to the chairperson.
2	The chairperson can review the minutes before sending them out to the voting participants. **Note:** the non-voting participants may not be privy to all of the messages that the chairperson sent out.
3	The voting participants review the minutes by comparing them to the emails that they received.
4	If the participants detect any errors, they should notify the chairperson for corrections.
5	The chairperson or secretary would make any corrections necessary before sending out the final copy of the minutes either in electronic or hard copy form.
6	Once the participants receive the final copy of the minutes they can delete the emails of the meeting.

Continued on next page

4.2.0. The Role of Secretary, Continued

4.2.4. Deleting emails of the meeting	It is customary for participants to delete the emails related to the meeting once they receive a copy of the final minutes. They do this for the following reasons.

- To save space on their computers.

- To prevent unauthorised access to the emails of the meeting.

- To make it easier to set up inbox rules in their email program for the next meeting.

4.2.5. Attachments	The minutes should have attached to it the original signed copy of the following.

1. Committee Reports

2. Officers Reports

3. Written Motions

4. Tellers Reports

5. Correspondence

4.3.0. The Role of Teller

**4.3.1.
Introduction**

The teller is the person who receives and counts the vote of the participants. This person could be:

- The chairperson — if the committee is small and has only a few motions

- Another participant

- Someone outside of the committee.

**4.3.2
Tabulating the
vote**

This table outlines the actions of chairpersons in their role as teller in tabulating votes.

Step	Action
1	Receives the votes.
2	Tabulates the votes.
3	Submits the results.

If the teller is...	Then the teller...
The speaker	Sends out the results email.
Not the speaker	Submits the results to the speaker for distribution.

4.4.0. Role of the Participants

4.4.1. Introduction	Just as face-to-face meeting have rules regarding decorum and etiquette, so do email meetings. These rules help to regulate the orderly flow of discussion.

4.4.2. General rules of etiquette

The following are the general rules of etiquette that apply for all email messages including email meetings.

- You should always assume that mail on the Internet is not secure; therefore do not put in an email message anything you would not put on a postcard. If the topic is of a sensitive nature, consider if an email meeting is the proper form to be using.

- In general, most people who are participating do not have time to answer general questions about the Internet and its workings. Do not send unsolicited mail asking for such information to committee members. Know who to contact for help.

- Remember that the location of the committee members could be anywhere in the world. If you send a message, do not expect an immediate response, the person receiving it might be at home asleep when it arrives, on vacation or in another time zone. Give them a chance to wake up, come to work, and log in before assuming the mail did not arrive or that they do not care.

- Remember that the recipient is a human whose culture, language, and humour may have different points of reference from your own. Be especially careful with sarcasm. Also, some date formats, measurements, and idioms may not travel well.

- Use mixed case. UPPER CASE LOOKS AS IF YOU ARE SHOUTING.

- Be conservative in the messages you send and liberal in what you receive. Do not send heated messages even if others provoke you. On the other hand, you should not be surprised if you get these. When you do receive a rude message, it is prudent not to respond to it.

- Do not include control characters or non-ASCII attachments in messages unless you are sure your recipient can decode them. Some systems may insert square boxes in the place of these characters while others leave the characters out, which can change the meaning of the message.

Continued on next page

4.4.0. Role of the Participants, Continued

4.4.2. General rules of etiquette, continued	• "Reasonable" expectations for conduct via email depends on your relationship to a person and the context of the communication. Norms learned in a particular email environment may not apply in general to your email communication with people across the Internet. Be careful with slang or local acronyms. For email meetings, always use a formal context.

4.4.3. Do's for email meetings

The following are the things you should do while participating in an email meeting.

- Sent meeting emails directly to the chairperson or speaker. It is his or her task to send out the messages in their proper order using the official distribution list. Skipping over the speaker can result in the other participants not receiving or ignoring your comments.

- Be brief without being overly terse. When replying to a message, include enough original material so that the speaker can understand, but no more. Remember, the speaker can cut material repeated unnecessarily. Edit out all the irrelevant material makes their jobs easier.

- Your messages to the speaker should have a subject heading which reflects its content. It should include the code identifying the meeting and, if appropriate, the order number.

- Know the size of your message. Sending large files may make your message so big that the Internet cannot deliver it. As a rule of thumb, never attach a file (or a combination of files) larger than 5 megabytes in a single message.

- Try to set aside time each day to participate in email meetings and remember to vote. This practice can keep you up to date on what is going on.

- Use spelling and grammar checking software, and proofread your message before you send it to the speaker.

- Include a signature so the speaker can quickly identify you when he or she forwards your message.

Continued on next page

4.4.0. Role of the Participants, Continued

4.4.4. Do not's for email meetings

The following are the things you should not do while participating in a meeting.

1. Do not forward or post to a website any message you have received as part of the meeting. Not even to the other committee members, with the only exception being the speaker. Always regard an email meeting as confidential.

2. Do not send the Speaker lengthy statements (more than 100 lines or 1,000 words). Members are unlikely to read and understand long messages. Keep your messages short by sticking to the point.

4.4.5. Other email rules

The following are the general rules of etiquette that apply for all email messages but are not applicable for email meeting, as your speaker should be weeding them out.

- Respect the copyright on material that you reproduce. Almost every country has copyright laws.

- If you are forwarding or re-posting a message you have received:
    - Do not change the wording. You may shorten the message and quote only relevant parts, but be sure you give proper attribution.
    - If the message was a personal message to you and you are re-posting to a group, you should ask permission first from the sender.
    - Beware the dreaded forwarding loop. Be sure you have not set up forwarding on several hosts so that a message sent to you gets into an endless loop from one computer to the next then back to the first computer.

- Never send chain letters via email. Internet service providers forbid chain letters, and they may revoke your network privileges. Notify your local system administrator if you ever receive one.

- It is a good idea to check all your mail subject lines from a sender before responding to their message. Sometimes a person who asks you for help (or clarification) may send another message, which effectively says "Never Mind."

Continued on next page

4.4.0. Role of the Participants, Continued

4.4.5. Other email rules, continued

- Watch out for carbon copies (cc). Make sure that you respond only to messages that the sender directed to you. If you receive a carbon copy (cc) message, consider giving time for the primary recipient to respond.

- To ensure that people know who you are, include a line or two at the end of your message with contact information.

- Be careful when addressing mail to make sure that the message is going to the correct person.
    - If you have 2 people in your contact list with the same or similar names, consider adding a middle initial or some other unique identifier to prevent the wrong person from receiving a message intended for the other.
    - Beware of addresses that looks like it is just one person, but goes to a group. Always know to whom you are sending a message.
    - Watch carbon copy (cc) when replying to a message. Do not continue to include people if the messages have become a 2-way conversation.
    - Verify all addresses before initiating personal discourse.

- Use an emoticon to indicate the tone of voice, but use them sparingly. Do not assume that the inclusion of a smiley face emoticon can make the recipient happy with what you said or wipe out an otherwise insulting comment.

- Just as postal mail may not be private, emails are subject to forgery and spoofing of various degrees of detectability. Apply common sense "reality checks" before assuming a message is valid. These checks include spelling, grammar, and general format. Ask yourself would the sender I know make this mistake, use that word or format the message this way.

- If you think the importance of a message justifies it, immediately send a brief reply to let the sender know you got it, and when they can expect you to send a longer reply later.

5.0.0. Organising Email Meetings

Overview

5.0.1. Introduction	As with any meeting, the facilitator or chairperson must organise an email meeting with the goal of getting the business done. This section looks at the terms used and options to consider when organising an email meeting.
5.0.2. Session	A session is a period that a committee allows for an email meeting. Depending on the purpose of the meeting, it can run anywhere from a few hours to over a year. Typically, sessions run either for the mandate of the committee (from one period of appointment or election to the next) or the period between face-to-face meetings. It takes its name from the periods, which divide a parliament.
5.0.3. Sitting	A sitting is a period over which the committee schedules its activities. Typically, a sitting runs for a week with the first day being for the introduction of motions and the last day for voting.
5.0.4. Cycle	A cycle is a schedule for the moving debating and voting on main motions; thus fixing the voting times for main motions. Typically, a cycle begins at the start of a sitting and ends at the end of the sitting; however, more than one cycle could occur within a sitting and cycles could extend over 2 or more sittings, depending on the committee's standing rules or motions to extend debate.

6.0.0. Main Motions and Statements

Overview

6.0.1.
Introduction

The chairperson organises email meeting discussions using threads. There are 2 types of threads.

- **Statements** — Comments and discussions on a topic, which begins with an invitation to comment and ends with a summary statement also referred to as a Communiqué; and

- **Motions** — Matters brought before the assembly that requires a vote, which begins with the motion and ends with the declaration announcing the results of the vote.

6.0.2.
Statements

We refer to messages that are not motions or address motions that are on the table as statements. The chairperson sends these messages out in 1 of following types of statement threads.

- **The Main Statement** — This thread contains all the messages related to the meeting.

- **Subject Statements** — These threads organise the information tabled by the members by the topics that members frequently comment on. The chairperson can set up separate threads for each topic.

The chairperson usually sends out statements from members in the order received.

Note: Statements are neither debatable nor amendable.

6.0.3.
Mandatory vote rule

It is mandatory for the mover or amender of a motion to vote for the motion. This rule serves the following purposes.

- It ensures that the teller records the vote of the mover of the motion if technical or other issues prevent the mover from casting their vote.

- It also prevents participants from delaying the timely resolution of a motion using amendments or division of a motion.

Continued on next page

Overview, Continued

Contents   This section contains the following topics:

6.1.0. Motions

6.1.1. **Introduction**	The chairperson sends out motion messages based on the order received. Different types of messages can find their way into a motion thread. This section lists these messages in the order of priority.

6.1.2. Appeals of motions

Purpose: Submit matter to members
Subject Line: #Appeal of the Motion to...
You Write: I appeal the decision of the chair to...
Debatable: Yes
Amendable: No
Vote: Majority
Note: The participant submits the motion for debate to the chairperson and vote in the next sitting.

6.1.3. Modifying motions

Purpose: Modify wording of the motion
Subject Line: #Amendment to the Motion
You Write: I move to amend the motion by...
Debatable: Yes
Amendable: Yes
Vote: Majority
Notes:

- If the proposer of the original motion modifies it, then the main motion is changed.

- If the proposer of the original motion does not propose the amendment, the chairperson places the amended motion as an option on the ballot and requires a majority to pass.

- If the amendment fails to gain a majority, then the teller adds the votes cast for the amendment to the original motion.

- Because of the mandatory vote rule, it is better to vote against a motion that you cannot live with than to try to amend it and hope to win a majority.

Continued on next page

6.1.0. Motions, Continued

6.1.4. Dividing motions	**Purpose:** Divide the motion **Subject Line:** #Divide the Motion **You Write:** I move to divide the question as follows. **Debatable:** No **Amendable:** Yes **Vote:** Majority **Notes:**

- Proposers of the original motions cannot make motions to divide a motion if it results in them exceeding their allotment of motions for the sitting.

- The chairperson can reject the motion to divide if the passage of the divisions does not have the same effect as the passage of the original motion.

- Because of the mandatory vote rule, both the parts of the divided the motion can have no fewer than 2 votes (the vote of the original maker and the divider); therefore, anyone wanting to divide a motion to make one part easier to defeat should have second thoughts.

- The chairperson replaces the original motion with the dividend motion on the ballot. However, if both motions of the division pass, then the secretary records the original motion as passing.

6.1.5. Speaking for motions	**Purpose:** To speak for the motion **Subject Line:** #For the Motion **You Write:** I am for the motion because… **Debatable:** No **Amendable:** No **Vote:** NA

6.1.6. Speaking against motions	**Purpose:** To speak against the motion **Subject Line:** #Against the Motion **You Write:** I am against the motion because… **Debatable:** No **Amendable:** No **Vote:** NA

Continued on next page

6.1.0. Motions, Continued

6.1.7. Making a motion	**Purpose:** Bring business before the assembly (a main motion) **Subject Line:** #Motion to… **You Write:** I move the following motion. Whereas… Be it resolved… **Debatable:** Yes **Amendable:** Yes **Vote:** Majority
6.1.8. Receiving a submission	**Purpose:** Bring a submission before the assembly (a main motion) **Subject Line:** #Submission From… **The Speaker Writes:** We have received the following motion from…. Whereas… Be it resolved… **Debatable:** Yes **Amendable:** Yes **Vote:** Majority
6.1.9. Invitation to vote	**Purpose:** To notify the members that it is time to vote on a motion or a submission **Subject Line:** #Vote **The Speaker Writes:** Voting on the motion to… **Debatable:** No **Amendable:** No **Vote:** Various
6.1.10. Announcing results	**Purpose:** To notify the members of the results of a vote on a motion or a submission **Subject Line:** #Results **The Speaker (or Teller) Writes:** The result of the vote on the motion is as follows. **Debatable:** No **Amendable:** No **Vote:** No

6.2.0. Main Statement

6.2.1. Introduction	The main statement thread contains all the messages related to the meeting. This section lists these messages in the order of appearance.

6.2.2. Beginning a session

Purpose: To establish a session
Subject Line: #Statement on this Session
The Chairperson Writes: I invite you to this session.
Note: The chairperson writes this statement.

6.2.3. Questions on rules

Purpose: Parliamentary law question
Subject Line: #Inquiry Regarding…
You Write: Parliamentary inquiry regarding…
Note: The chairperson would answer the question in a separate message with the subject line "#Answer Regarding…."

6.2.4. Request to enforce rules

Purpose: Enforce rules
Subject Line: #Point of Order
The Chairperson Writes: Point of Order regarding…
Note: The chairperson would acknowledge the request in a separate message by either:

- Reminding the participants of the rules; or

- Explaining that the chairperson has enforced the rules.

6.2.5. Complaints

Purpose: Register complaint
Subject Line: #Complaint Regarding
You Write: I wish to register a question of privilege regarding…
Note: The chairperson would acknowledge the complaint in a separate message.

6.2.6. Ending a session

Purpose: To acknowledge the end of a session
Subject Line: #Final Communiqué
The Chairperson Writes: The summary of the session is as follows
Note: The chairperson writes this statement summarising the business of the session by listing the motions passed.

6.3.0. Subject Statement

6.3.1. Introduction	A subject statement thread contains all the messages related to a particular subject. The chairperson should set up separate subject statement threads as soon as the session starts for those topics that members are likely to discuss. The chairperson can always add additional threads whenever a new subject comes up. This section lists subject statement messages in the order that they would appear in a subject statement thread.
6.3.2. Invitation to comment	**Purpose:** To establish a subject for comment **Subject Line:** #Statement on… **The Speaker Writes:** I invite you to comment on… **Notes:** • The speaker would generally write the invitation to comment, but a member who introduced the subject could also write the message. • The message should include a summary of the topic.
6.3.3. Tabling reports	**Purpose:** To table a report **Subject Line:** #Report on… **You Write:** Attached is a report on… **Note:** When the report is an attachment to the message, the member introducing the report should provide a summary of the report.
6.3.4. Requests for information	**Purpose:** Request for information **Subject Line:** #Request for Information Regarding… **You Write:** Point of information regarding… **Note:** Participants should be specific as possible about the information that they require.

Continued on next page

6.3.0. Subject Statement, Continued

6.3.5. Response to information request	**Purpose:** To respond to a requested for information **Subject Line:** #Response Regarding… **You Write:** My response to the request for information regarding… **Notes:** • Participants should promptly submit responses to the chairperson. • When someone needs more time for a response, he or she should let everyone know when to expect a response through the chairperson.
6.3.6. Commenting	**Purpose:** To comment on a subject **Subject Line:** #Comment Regarding… **You Write:** My thoughts regarding… **Note:** Participants should ensure that their comments are useful to the other members and reframe from expressing their opinion without providing a unique or fresh idea.
6.3.7. Summarising statements	**Purpose:** To summarise a statement **Subject Line:** #Communiqué… **The chairperson Writes:** A summary of this subject is as follows. **Notes:** The chairperson: • May prepare a summarising statement during a session when the thread has a large volume of messages. • Usually prepares a summarising statement at the end of the session.

6.4.0. Out Dated Motions

6.4.1. Introduction	There are several motions common in a face-to-face meeting, but not used in an email meeting.
6.4.2. Motion to adjourn	*Motion to adjourn* – Participants would use this motion to halt the session leaving any business before the assembly unfinished. Since participants cannot end an email meeting before its closing date as announced in the call, this motion is not appropriate.
6.4.3. Motion to recess	*Motion to recess* – Participants would use this motion so that they can take a break from the meeting. Since participants do not miss any of the meetings if they take a break from their computer, we do not need this motion.
6.4.4. Limit debate	*Limit debate*—Participants would use this motion to close debate at a fixed time or limit debate for a certain period thus preventing debate from dragging out. Since the sitting period determents when a vote occurs, this motion would be redundant.
6.4.5. Extend debate	*Extend debate*—Participants would use this motion to extend debate until a fixed time or a certain period in the hopes of being able to persuade the other side to their way of thinking. The chairperson can give members a choice when voting on the main motion to extend the debate into the next session, making this motion unnecessary. To prevent the debate from dragging on, if a clear majority is not in favour of extending the debate, any votes cast for extension are re-casted in the negative. Therefore, the only reason to vote for an extension is the hope that something would come up that would cause the member to vote for the motion.
6.4.6. Refer to committee	*Refer to committee*—Chairperson would use this motion to move items to a smaller more manageable group for study and report. However, because of the nature of email meetings, each member has plenty of time to do research on issues and report to the committee.

Continued on next page

6.4.0. Out Dated Motions, Continued

6.4.7. Kill main motion

Kill main motion—Participants would use this motion to stop a motion that was found to be without merit so that others motions could be tables. Since a committee can consider a multitude of motions at the same time in an email meeting, there is no harm in a committee considering a motion that has no merit and voting it down.

6.4.8. Ready to vote

Ready to vote—Participants would use this motion to hasten the vote on a motion. Since the sitting period determines the when voting occurs, this motion would be redundant

7.0.0. Examples

Overview

**7.0.1.
Introduction**

To illustrate how the rules for email meetings work let us look at a hypnotical organisation that operates internationally over the Intranet.

**7.0.2 Email
Chess
Federation**

Our hypnotical organisation, the Email Chess Federation (ECF), matches players from around the world who play chess with each other using email. While it has several committees, for the purpose of our examples we will only be looking at the Board of Directors (B).

The Board (B) has 12 members from around the world. They are responsible for the oversite of the whole Federation. Their sessions run annually beginning 1 April. Their sittings begin on Monday and end on Sunday.

The board has the following officers.

- Premier

- Speaker

- Teller

- Secretary

- Treasurer

Contents

This section contains the following topics:

7.1.0. Main Statement Examples

**7.1.1.
Introduction**

This section illustrations some of the messages that would be in the main statement thread. With a few edits, a speaker can cut and paste most of these statements into the email message for the next session.

**7.1.2 Beginning
a session**

The following is an example of the main statement to begin a session.

From:	Speaker <Speaker@IECF.com>
Sent:	March 16, 2016 4:50 PM
To:	ECF Board
Subject:	ECF-B-2016-001: #Statement on this Session

I invite you to this session of the Email Chess Federation's Board of Directors for 2016.

I will be sending out the messages for this meeting with the subject line beginning with "EFC-B-2016-." I suggest either setting up an inbox rule or modify your current rule in your Email program to organise your messages regarding this meeting.

When sending messages to me regarding this meeting, please remember that your messages will be sent back unread if any one of the following rules are not followed.

• The message must be sent only to the Speaker of the Board's Email Address — SpeakerOfTheBoard@EmailChessFed.com

• The subject line of the message must begin with "EFC-B-2016."

• Your message contains unparliamentary language.

Please include the thread number in the subject line when responding to a statement or motion so I can place it in the right thread.

Our sitting will run from Monday to Sunday, and our session will end on the last Sunday of 2016.

Jane Doe
Speaker of the Board

Continued on next page

7.1.0. Main Statement Examples, Continued

7.1.3 Question on rules

The following is an example of the question on the rules to a speaker.

From:	John Smith <JohnSmith@IECF.com>
Sent:	March 16, 2016 4:50 PM
To:	Speaker <Speaker@IECF.com>
Subject:	ECF-B-2016-001: # Inquiry Regarding My Motion

Parliamentary inquiry regarding my motion.

I submitted a motion on Monday, but there is still no thread. Did you receive it?

John Smith

7.1.4 Response to a question on rules

The following is an example of a response to a question on the rules.

From:	Speaker <Speaker@IECF.com>
Sent:	March 16, 2016 4:50 PM
To:	ECF Board
Subject:	ECF-B-2016-001: #Answer Regarding My Motion

Mr Smith, I did receive your motion, but you missed the deadline of Friday. It will be in the next sitting of the Board.

Jane Doe
Speaker of the Board

Continued on next page

7.1.0. Main Statement Examples, Continued

7.1.5 Ending a session

The following is an example of how the speaker would end a session.

From:	Speaker <Speaker@IECF.com>
Sent:	March 16, 2016 4:50 PM
To:	ECF Board
Subject:	ECF-B-2016-001: #Close the Session

The summary of the session is as follows.

001 Main Statement
002 Rules Committee Statement
003 Appeals Committee Statement
004 Administration Statement
005 Motion to Approve Financial Statements (Carried)
006 Application to Change Appeals Policy

Jane Doe
Speaker of the Board

7.2.0. Subject Statement Examples

7.2.1. Introduction

This section illustrations some of the messages that would be in the subject statement thread.

7.2.2 Beginning a subject statement

The following is an example of how a speaker begins a subject statement thread.

From:	Speaker <Speaker@IECF.com>
Sent:	March 16, 2016 4:50 PM
To:	IECF Board
Subject:	ECF-B-2016-004: #Statements on Administration

I invite you to make comments regarding administration matters for this session with the subject line beginning with "EFC-B-2016-004."

When sending messages to me regarding administration, please include the thread number in the subject line when responding to a statement or motion so I can place it in the right thread.

Jane Doe
Speaker of the Board

Continued on next page

7.2.0. Subject Statement Examples, Continued

7.2.3 Tabling reports

The following is an example of how to submit a report to the speaker

From:	Susan Anthony <SusanAnthony@IECF.com>
Sent:	March 16, 2016 4:50 PM
To:	Speaker@IECF.com
Subject:	ECF-B-2016-004: #Report on Financial Statements

Attached are the financial statements for February 2016.

Reviewing the statements, I note the following.

• Cash on hand amounts to $12,463

• Revenue over expenses to date amounts to $2,952 (we are $952 over our budget projection of $2,000).

I'll be happy to answer any questions.

Susan Anthony
Treasurer

7.2.4 Request for information

The following is an example of how to submit a request for information.

From:	John Smith <JohnSmith@IECF.com>
Sent:	March 16, 2016 4:50 PM
To:	Speaker@IECF.com
Subject:	ECF-B-2016-004: #Request for Information on Sales Tax Rebate

Point of information regarding the financial statements, I cannot see where we received our sales tax rebate on the statement of operations. Did we receive this money?

John Smith

Continued on next page

7.2.0. Subject Statement Examples, Continued

7.2.5 Response with information

The following is an example of how to respond to a request for information.

From:	Susan Anthony <SusanAnthony@IECF.com>
Sent:	March 16, 2016 4:50 PM
To:	Speaker@IECF.com
Subject:	ECF-B-2016-004: #Response to Question on Sales Tax Rebate

My response to the request for information regarding a question on the sales tax rebate is as follows. I have applied for and received the sales tax rebate. Because the accounting entry originally recorded as a receivable and we received the rebate by year's end thus reversing the receivable. On the statement of operations, the related expenses would have been reduced by the amount of the rebate. Thus there would not be a separate line item for the rebate.

Susan Anthony
Treasurer

7.2.6 Comment

The following is an example of how to make a comment on a subject.

From:	John Smith <JohnSmith@IECF.com>
Sent:	March 16, 2016 4:50 PM
To:	Speaker@IECF.com
Subject:	ECF-B-2016-004: #Comment Regarding the Financial Statements

My thoughts regarding our cash position being down $1,000 from last year is because we had to replace one of the servers.

John Smith

Continued on next page

7.2.0. Subject Statement Examples, Continued

**7.2.7
Summarising
statement**

The following is an example of how to summarise a subject thread.

From:	Speaker <Speaker@IECF.com>
Sent:	March 16, 2016 4:50 PM
To:	Speaker@IECF.com
Subject:	ECF-B-2016-004: #Communiqué on Administration

A summary of this subject is as follows.

• Ms Anthony submitted the financial statements for February 2016.

• We have received our sales tax rebate, which Ms Anthony has recorded as a reduction in expenses.

• Our cash position is down by $1,000 because we replaced a server.

Jane Doe
Speaker of the Board

7.3.0. Example of a Motion

7.3.1. Introduction	This section illustrations some of the messages that the speaker would send when someone makes a motion.

7.3.2 Making a motion	The following is an example of how to make a main motion.

> **From:** Susan Anthony <SusanAnthony@IECF.com>
> **Sent:** March 16, 2016 4:50 PM
> **To:** Speaker@IECF.com
> **Subject:** ECF-B-2016: #Motion to Approve Financial Statements
>
> I move the following motion.
>
> *Be it resolved that the financial statements as tabled be approved.*
>
> Susan Anthony
> Treasurer

Note: When making a motion, do not add an order number. The speaker will assign an order number in the subject line as this when he or she sends out the motion.

7.3.3 Speaking against the motion	The following is an example of how to speak against a motion.

> **From:** John Smith <JohnSmith@IECF.com>
> **Sent:** March 16, 2016 4:50 PM
> **To:** Speaker@IECF.com
> **Subject:** ECF-B-2016-005: #Against the Motion
>
> I am against the motion because the sales tax rebate should be shown separately on the financial statements.
>
> John Smith

Continued on next page

7.3.0. Example of a Motion, Continued

7.3.4 Speaking for a motion

The following is an example of how to speak for a motion.

From:	Susan Anthony < SusanAnthony@IECF.com>
Sent:	March 16, 2016 4:50 PM
To:	Speaker@IECF.com
Subject:	ECF-B-2016-005: #For the Motion

I am for the motion because showing expenses net of sales taxes is an acceptable way of presenting financial information on the statement of operations.

Susan Anthony
Treasurer

7.3.5 Dividing a motion

The following is an example of how to request that a motion be divided.

From:	John Smith <JohnSmith@IECF.com>
Sent:	March 16, 2016 4:50 PM
To:	Speaker@IECF.com
Subject:	ECF-B-2016-005: #Divide the Motion

I move to divide the motion as follows.

- *Be it resolved that the statement of financial position as tabled be approved.*

- *Be it resolved that the statement of operations as tabled be approved.*

John Smith

Continued on next page

7.3.0. Example of a Motion, Continued

7.3.6 Modifying a motion

The following is an example of how to request that a motion be modified.

From:	John Smith <JohnSmith@IECF.com>
Sent:	March 16, 2016 4:50 PM
To:	Speaker@IECF.com
Subject:	ECF-B-2016-005: #Amendment to the Motion

I move to amend the motion as follows.

Be it resolved, that the financial statements as tabled be approved <u>subject to the approval of our auditors.</u>

John Smith

7.3.7 Appeals of motion

The following is an example of how to appeal a motion.

From:	Susan Anthony <SusanAnthony@IECF.com>
Sent:	March 16, 2016 4:50 PM
To:	Speaker@IECF.com
Subject:	ECF-B-2016-005: #Appeal of Motion to Divide Motion

I appeal the decision of the chair to allow John to divide the motion, as the Board must approve the financial statements as a whole.

Susan Anthony
Treasurer

Continued on next page

7.3.0. Example of a Motion, Continued

7.3.8 Invitation to vote   The following is an example of how a speaker would invite everyone to vote.

From:	Speaker <Speaker@IECF.com>
Sent:	March 18, 2016 4:50 PM
To:	IECF Board
Subject:	ECF-B-2016-005: #Vote

Voting on the motion to approve the financial statements is now opened. You have until March 20, 2016, at 11:59 pm to submit your vote. Use the voting button in this message to cast your vote and to send it to the teller.

Jane Doe
Speaker of the Board

Continued on next page

7.3.0. Example of a Motion, Continued

**7.3.9
Announcing
results**

The following is an example of how to the teller would report vote results to the speaker.

From:	Sally Cove <SallyCove@IECF.com>
Sent:	March 21, 2016 4:50 PM
To:	Speaker@IECF.com
Subject:	ECF-B-2016-005: #Results

The result of the vote on the motion is as follows.

- *Be it resolved, that the statement of financial position as tabled be approved.*
  - For 4
  - Against 0

- *Be it resolved, that the statement of operations as tabled be approved.*
  - For 3
  - Against 1

Result: Be it resolved, that the financial statements as tabled be approved. (3 for the motion 1 against.)

Explanation of results: The original motion passed because both parts of the divided motion passes.

Sally Cove
Teller of the Board

7.4.0. Example of a Submission

**7.4.1.
Introduction**

This section illustrations some of the messages that would be in a submissions thread.

**7.4.2
Submission
motion**

The following is an example of how the speaker introduces a submission.

From:	Speaker <Speaker@IECF.com>
Sent:	March 16, 2016 4:50 PM
To:	IECF Board
Subject:	ECF-B-2016-006: # Submission From the Appeals Committee Regarding Policy Change

We have received the following motion from the Appeals Committee regarding a change to the appeals policy.

Whereas, there is a need for impartiality in reviewing appeals.

Be it resolved, that the name, location, and other identifying references be removed from appeal applications before it is submitted to an adjudicator.

A copy of the revised policy is attached to this message.

Jane Doe
Speaker of the Board

Continued on next page

7.4.0. Example of a Submission, Continued

7.4.3 Invitation to vote

The following is an example of how the speaker invites everyone to vote on a submission.

From:	Speaker <Speaker@IECF.com>
Sent:	March 18, 2016 4:50 PM
To:	IECF Board
Subject:	ECF-B-2016-006: #Vote

Voting on the submission from the Appeals Committee regarding a policy change is now opened. You have until March 20, 2016, at 11:59 pm to submit your vote to me. Use the voting button in this message to cast your vote and to send it to the teller.

Jane Doe
Speaker of the Board

7.4.4 Announcement of results

The following is an example of how the teller reports the results to the speaker.

From:	Sally Cove <SallyCove@IECF.com>
Sent:	March 21, 2016 4:50 PM
To:	Speaker@IECF.com
Subject:	ECF-B-2016-006: #Results

The results of the vote on the motion is as follows.

Be it resolved, that the name, location, and other identifying references be removed from appeal applications before it is submitted to an adjudicator.

- For 6

- Against 0

Result: Motion carried.

Sally Cove
Teller of the Board

Definitions

Terms

Bylaws	A bylaw is a rule or law established by an organisation or community to regulate itself, as allowed or provided for by some higher authority.
Distribution list	A distribution list is a collection of contacts or addresses. It provides an easy way to send Email messages to a group of people. A message sent to a distribution list goes to all recipients listed in the distribution list. In Microsoft Outlook, you can include distribution lists in messages, task requests, meeting requests, and even in other distribution lists.
Deliberative assembly	A deliberative assembly is a gathering of members who use parliamentary procedure to make decisions.
Inbox rules	Inbox rules are instructions that you set up within an email program that performs certain actions on messages for which you have set certain permissions. It is a way to manage your messages automatically. You set up an inbox rule in the program, so when you send a message (or when a message arrives in your mailbox), the inbox rule executes the required actions.
Premier	A premier is the chief officer of a deliberative assembly where there is a speaker runs the email meeting.
Quorum	A quorum is the minimum number of members of a deliberative assembly necessary to conduct the business of that group. The requirement for a quorum is protection against unrepresentative actions in the name of the body by an unduly small number of people.
Speaker	The speaker is an officer of a deliberative assembly where there is a premier.

Bibliography

References

Berleant, D., & Liu, B. (1995, November). *Robert's Rules of Order for e-mail meetings*. (R. Vetter, Ed.) Retrieved February 6, 2016, from Computer: Internet Kiosk: http://ualr.edu/jdberleant/papers/email-meetings.html

Kennedy, B. (1997). *Robert's Rules of Order - Summary Version*. Retrieved April 30, 2014, from Robert's Rules of Order: http://www.robertsrules.org/

Robert's Rules of Order. (n.d.). *Robert's Rules of Order Motions Chart*. Retrieved April 30, 2014, from Robert's Rules of Order: http://www.robertsrules.org/motions.htm

Stackpole, J. (2003, April). Bylaws for E-Meetings. *Parliamentary Journal, Volume XLIV*(Number 2).Stackpole, J. D. (2001, July). Rules for Electronic (e-mail) Meetings. *Parliamentary Journal, Volume XLII*(Number 3).

Stackpole, J. D. (2001, July). Rules for Electronic (e-mail) Meetings. *Parliamentary Journal, Volume XLII*(Number 3).

Stackpole, J. D. (2002, April). A Response to James Stewart's Comments on E-Voting. *Parliamentary Journal, Volume XLIII*(Number 2).

Stewart, J. H. (2002). Voting in Electronic Meetings. *Parliamentary Journal, Volume XLIII*(Number 2).

Sylvester, N. (2000). E-Meeting – the Future Is NOW! *National Parliamentarian*(Second Quarter).

Sylvester, N. (2001). E-Meeting-The Future Is Now! Part II. *National Parliamentarian*(First Quarter).

The Institute of Electrical and Electronics Engineers, Inc. (2003). *Best Practices for Conducting Meetings by Email*. Retrieved February 6, 2016, from IEEE: http://www.ieee.org/about/corporate/governance/email_meetings.html

www.ingramcontent.com/pod-product-compliance
Lightning Source LLC
Chambersburg PA
CBHW081748220526
45468CB00008B/2293